how long has this been going on

VAN MORRISON with georgie fame & friends

This publication is not authorised for sale in the United States of America and/or Canada

Distributors:
Music Sales Limited
8/9 Frith Street, London W1V 5TZ, England.
Music Sales Pty Limited
120 Rothschild Avenue, Rosebery, NSW2018, Australia.
Order No. AM939060
ISBN 0-7119-5953-6
Visit the Music Sales' Internet Music Shop at
http://www.musicsales.co.uk

International Music Publications Limited
Southend Road, Woodford Green, Essex IG8 8HN, England.
International Music Publications Limited
25 Rue D'Hauteville, 75010 Paris, France.
International Music Publications Gmbh, Germany
Marstallstrasse 8, D-80539 Munchen.
Order Ref. 4375A
ISBN 1-85909-396-5

Music arranged by Jack Long
Music processed by Paul Ewers Music Design

Printed in the United Kingdom by
Caligraving Limited, Thetford, Norfolk.

Wise Publications
London / New York / Sydney / Copenhagen / Madrid

International Music Publications Limited
Southend Road, Woodford Green, Essex IG8 8HN, England

i will be there

Words & Music by Van Morrison

1. When-ev-er the sun-shine comes through,— when-ev-er my thoughts turn to

(Verse 2 Instrumental: ad lib., no stops)

you,— what-ev-er you want me to do,—

the new symphony sid

Words & Music by King Pleasure and Lester Young

To Coda ⊕

1.

2.

3. Tune in and lis-ten, check what you're
(Verse 4 ad lib. instrumental)

miss-in'. You'll find it close to eight-y on— the dial.

Some say he's the great-est, one thing is for sure: when you hear the lat-est,

you're gon-na be hop-pin' and bop-pin' round the kit-chen. All— your friends—

Sis - ters and bro - thers, fa - thers and mo - thers, dig - gin'—

1. **2.** **D.%. al Coda**
(Instrumental)

what— Sid's— put - - - tin' down.—

⊕ *Coda*

Sym - pho - ny Sid— is jump - in',

Sym - pho - ny Sid.—

11

early in the morning

Words & Music by Leo Hickman, Louis Jordan & Dallas Bartley

1. Ear-ly in the morn-ing, an' I can't___ get right.___
(Verses 2, 3, 4, 5 & 6 see block lyric)

Had a lit-tle date with my ba-by last night.___ Now it's ear-ly in the morn-ing,

13

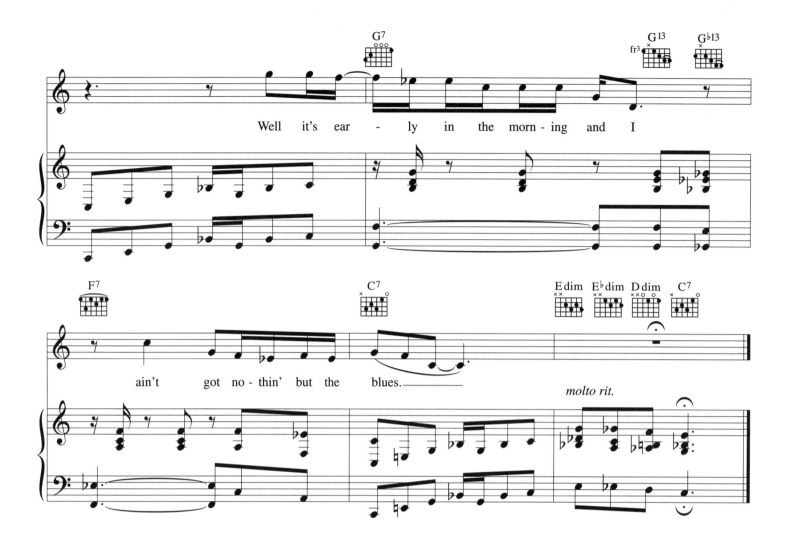

Well it's ear - ly in the morn - ing and I

ain't got no - thin' but the blues.

molto rit.

Verse 2:

Went to all the places where we used to go.
Went to her house, but she don't live there no mo'.
Now it's early in the morning,
Now it's early in the morning.
Early in the morning,
And I ain't got nothin' but the blues.

Verse 3:

Went to her girlfriend's house, but she was out.
Knocked on her father's door, and he began to shout.
Early in the morning,
Early in the morning.
Early in the morning.
And I ain't got nothin' but the blues.

Verse 4:
Ad lib. instrumental

Verse 5:
Ad lib. instrumental

Verse 6:

Went to Doogie J's to get something to eat;
Waiter looked at me and said "You sure look beat."
And it's early in the morning,
Early in the morning.
Well it's early in the morning,
And I ain't got nothin' but the blues.

14

who can i turn to?

Words & Music by Leslie Bricusse & Anthony Newley

heart wants to go
(s *ad lib. instrumental*)

so I must know

where my des-ti-ny leads me._____

No

star to guide me,

and no_____ one be-side me,

I will go on my way

and af-ter the day_____

the

I could cling to,   I can learn to with you   on one of them new

— days.   Who can   I turn to   if you   turn a - way?

18

Verse 2:
Maybe tomorrow I will find what I'm after.
I wanna beg, steal or borrow my share of laughter.
With you, I could learn to;
Oh baby with you,
With you on one of them new days.
Who can I turn to if you turn away?

sack o' woe

Music by Julian Adderley. Words by Jon Hendricks

(1, 10.) Hol - l'rin', scream - in' 'cos I'm suf - f'rin' so.___
(Verses 2, 4, 5, 7, 8, 11 see block lyric)

Life___ done___ dealt___ me such a ter - ri - ble blow.___

The bag I'm in is just a sack o' woe.

(3, 12.) Trou-ble's one thing I un-der-stand, seems to be a part of
(Verses 6 & 9 see block lyric)

me. Mis-'ry an' me go hand in hand,

never ever let me be. Sure as I'm born, one

Verse 3

thing I know:— the bag I'm in— is just a sack o' woe.—

Back to *

Verse 6   *Back to ** *Verse 9*   *Back to **

Verses 2 & 11:
Mis'ry got me an' I'm feelin' low.
Trouble follows me wherever I go.
The bag I'm in is just a sack o' woe.

Verses 4, 5, 6, 7, 8 & 9:
Ad lib. instrumental

moondance

Words & Music by Van Morrison

1. Well it's a mar-vel-lous night__ for a moon-dance,   with the
(Verse 2 see block lyric; Verses 3-7 ad lib. instrumental)

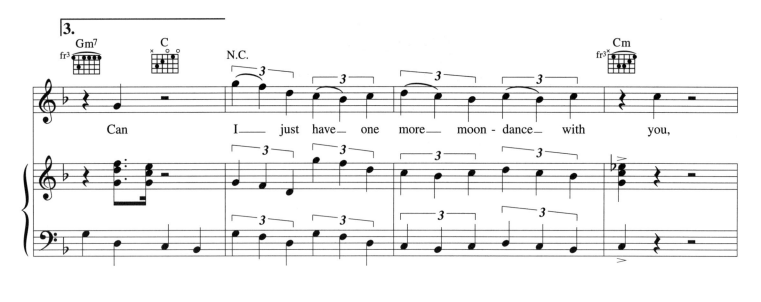

Can   I— just have— one   more— moon - dance— with   you,

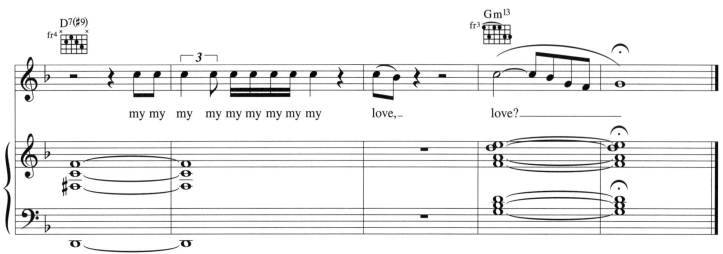

my my my   my my my my my my   love,—   love?_____

Verse 2:

Well I wanna make love to you tonight,
I can't wait till the morning has come.
And I know now the timing is just right,
And straight into my arms you will run.
And when you come my heart will be waiting
To make sure that you're never alone.
There and then all my dreams will come true dear;
There and then I will make you my own.
Every time I touch you, you just tremble inside.
And I know how much I want you baby,
That you can't hide.
Can I just have one more moondance with you, my love?
Can I just make some more romance with you, my love?

centerpiece
(incorporating blues backstage)

Centerpiece Music by Harry 'Sweets' Edison
Words by Jon Hendricks
Blues Backstage By Frank Foster

Verses 2 & 8:
I'll buy a house and garden somewhere
Along a country road a piece;
A little cottage on the outskirts,
Where we can really find release.
But nothing's any good without you;
'Cos, baby, you're my centerpiece.

Verses 3, 4 & 5: ad lib. instrumental

Verse 6: solo

how long has this been going on?

Music & Lyrics by George Gershwin & Ira Gershwin

1. I could cry salty tears; where have I been all these years? Little wow, tell me now:

How long has this been go - ing on?___

There ___ were chills___ up and down___ my spine.

There's some thrills___ I can't de - fine.___ Lis - ten, sweet, while

I re - peat:___ How long has this been go - ing on?___

Verse 2:
What a kick! How I buzz!
Boy, you click like no-one does!
Hear me, sweet, I'll take a peek.
How long has this been going on?

your mind is on vacation

Words & Music by Mose Allison

is on va-ca-tion and your mouth is work-in' ov-er-time.

You're quot-ing fig-ures,
(Verse 3 see block lyric)

you're drop-pin' names, you're tell-in' stor-ies, you're play-in' games.

You're al-ways laugh-in' when things ain't fun-ny; it's start-in' to sound like you don't

need mo-ney. Tough as a cri - mi-nal, you lead a life of crime.

'cos your mind is on va-ca-tion and your

mouth is work-in' ov-er - time.

Ad lib. instrumental

You know that

'Cos your mind___ is on va-ca-tion and your

Verse 2:
You know that life is short and talk is cheap.
Don't make promises that you can't keep.
If you don't like the song I'm singing, just grin and bear it.
All I can say is "If the shoe fits, wear it."
If you must keep talkin', please can you make it rhyme?
'Cos your mind is on vacation and your mouth is workin' overtime.

all saints' day

Words & Music by Van Morrison

2, 𝄋. You can make your re-ser-va-tion,
(5. Ad lib. instrumental)

I will meet you at the sta-tion when you come to see

me All Saints Day.

To Coda ⊕

(Vocal in, 5.) Fol-low her lead, it is

no won-der I seem to be so high;

liv- ing my dreams the way I ought to as the days go roll-

-ing by. 3. See me stroll- ing through the mea - dow
(Verse 6 see block lyric)

with you, ba - by, by the way. Won't you come to see

me All Saints Day?

1.   2.   *D.%. al Coda*

44

Verse 6:
See the streamlined blue horizon,
With you, baby, by the way.
Won't you come to see me
All Saints Day?

blues in the night (my mama done tol' me)

Words by Johnny Mercer
Music by Harold Arlen

1. My ma - ma done tol' me,_____ when

(Verses 2 & 3 see block lyric)

I was in knee-pants,__ my ma - ma done tol' me, "Son,_____ a

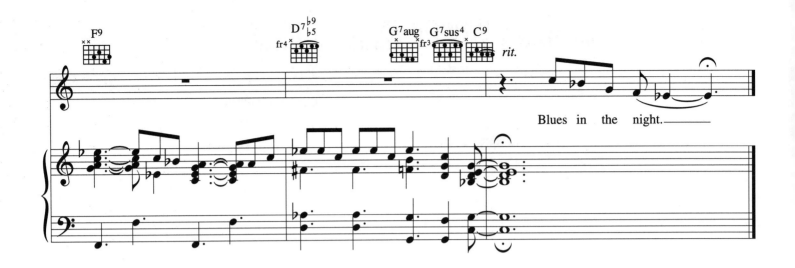

Blues in the night.—————

Verse 2:
Now the rain is fallin',
Hear the train a-callin',
"Whooee."
Hear the lonesome whistle
Blowin' across the trestle,
"Whooee,
Dooee doo doo di,
A-clickety-clack," go echoin' back,
The blues in the night.

Verse 3:
From Natchez to Mobile,
Memphis to St. Joe,
Wherever the four winds blow.
I've been in some big towns,
And heard me some big talk,
But there is one thing I know:
A woman's a two-faced,
A worrisome thing that'll leave you to sing
The blues in the night.

don't worry about a thing

Words & Music by Mose Allison

think, well I've got some con-so-la-tion:

I'll give it to you if I___ might.

You know I don't wor-ry a-bout a thing, be-cause

no-thing's gon-na turn out___ right.___

2. Well this

2.

Don't _ spend_____ your time try-in' to be a big win-ner, min-ute you get fat some-bo-dy else-'ll get thin-ner. There's al-ways some-bo-dy mess- -in' with dy-na-mite.____

Verse 2:
Well, this world's just one big trouble spot;
Some have plenty and some have not.
I used to be trouble,
But I fin'lly saw the light.
Now I don't worry about a thing,
Because I know nothing's gonna be alright.

that's life

Words & Music by Dean Kay & Kelly Gordon

life,   that's what the peo - ple   say;——————

(Verse 2 see block lyric; ℅ ad lib instrumental)

youre rid-in' high in A-pril,—— shot down in May.——

I know I've got—— to change— my tune—————— when I get back

1.

up on top—— in June.—————— 2. That's

2.

(Vocal in on %.)

world keeps— spin-nin' round. I've been a

Verse 2:
That's life, funny as it may seem;
Some people get their kicks from
Steppin' on a dream.
I don't let it get me down;
This big old world keeps spinnin' round.

heathrow shuffle

Words & Music by Van Morrison

(11.) Heath - row shuf - fle, Heath - row shuf - fle, yeah, ba ba doo day.

(Verses 5 & 8 ad lib. instrumental)

Heath - row shuf - fle, Heath - row shuf - fle,

yeah, ba ba doo day. Got - ta go to Heath - row,

got - ta - go to Heath - row, yeah, ba ba do day.